FIVE ARTISTS - FIVE DIRECTIONS IN POLYMER CLAY

by Jamey D. Allen

recent works by

Pier Voulkos

Martha Breen

Ruth Anne Grove

Michael Grove

and

Jamey D. Allen

1. Earrings *Fashion and Fusion* series. 3 1/2" long, applique technique. By Ruth Anne Grove.

ISBN 0-9620543-8-0

Photo Credits

All photos are by **George Post** with the exception of

21, 23, 24 and 25 by **Schuyler Pescada** and

2, 59, 60, 61, 65, 66, and 69 by **Jamey D. Allen**.

2. Detail of *Two Necklaces*. Combed and folded beads, in tones of black, white, and gray. By Jamey D. Allen. See page 46.

This book is fondly dedicated to

MY MOTHER

who always encouraged my art

INTRODUCTION

*Polymer Five is a casual consortium formed by five artists located in and around the San Francisco Bay Area in 1992: Pier Voulkos, Martha Breen (Urban Tribe), Michael and Ruth Anne Grove (Grove and Grove), and Jamey D. Allen. We five have been working with polymer clay for a number of years, and are among the main proponents of this not-quite-accepted and avant garde art form in the West. With the publication of Nan Roche's fabulous book, **The New Clay**, the polymer clays have quickly gained ground, respectability, and popularity. In addition, her book has instigated an amazing amount of networking between and among artists all over the country and the world. I first met Michael and Ruth Anne Grove in the Spring of 1992, at a meeting of the Northern California Bead Society where they were presenting a program on their work. We got together afterwards, and entered into an interesting discussion about our pursuits, and the medium – and we considered the possibility of organizing a group show that would feature the work of a few outstanding local artists. From this beginning, Michael Grove has been our primary organizer and motivator – choosing participants, arranging meetings, and finding exhibition space. Although we all think of* *ourselves as primarily jewelrymakers, we each were at a stage where we felt it was desirable to push the medium a step farther, to experiment with other forms – and to present this work to the public as well. Our first show, called Five Directions in Polymer opened at The Giorgi Gallery in Berkeley on May 7th, and was on view for nearly two months before moving on to other locations – Gallery Eight in La Jolla, California, and Twist Gallery in Portland, Oregon.*

Prior to our first Polymer Five meeting, I had just recently met Michael and Ruth Anne Grove, and had not yet made the acquaintance of either Pier Voulkos or Martha Breen – though I was familiar with their work for a long time. I think we were all somewhat surprised to find that we developed into a group that can honestly be characterized as having tremendous mutual respect. We liked the work we each were doing, and we all liked one another immediately. It was refreshingly pleasant to get together, and to discuss and plan our group exhibitions. I believe each of us feels his or her work is nicely complimented by association with the others. We have a lot in common, yet maintain a personal, distinctive look that is unique to each of us. In short, our association has been joyful. It has also been a challenge, in the sense that we committed ourselves to produce new work that went beyond the scope of past productions – already considered to be on the cutting edge of polymer clay art. We have tried to outdo ourselves, and have succeeded in surprising ways.

We received an offer to document our Five Directions in Polymer show, in the form of a book, from Flower Valley Press, and felt this was a great opportunity to share the work with a wider audience. Like many artists, we are loath to talk about ourselves very much. We prefer to present our work, and let it speak for itself. However, understanding that people are naturally curious about us as artists, and about the origins and development of our art, we have decided to present brief biographical sketches that will answer some of the questions we receive on a routine basis whenever such topics are discussed. To this end, I conducted interviews with each person asking them to talk about their approach to the medium, and to tell about past experiences and history that influenced the work being done today. We hope readers will find that this information satisfies their curiosity, and puts the work into perspective.

Since we began documenting our first group show, we have gone on to participate in another larger and more ambitious show on the subject of Masks and Mask Images – featuring eleven polymer clay artists from around the country. As I write, this second show is in transit between sites, and has been an exciting experience for all concerned. But that is another story.

Jamey D. Allen

3. *Before After but After Before* Polymer clay picture. 10" wide x 14" high by Michael Grove.

4. *Shaggy Red Frame.* 10" x 18" long, housing
a *Long Fancy Neckpiece. Pier Voulkos*

PIER VOULKOS

Pier Voulkos was born in Helena, Montana, on December 24, 1952 – the daughter of artists. Her father, Peter Voulkos, is a well-known ceramics sculptor; and her mother has been a potter and a teacher of ceramics and other crafts for many years. With such a background, there has never been a time when Pier was not involved in some art or craft. She attended the California College of Arts and Crafts between 1971 and 1975, and acquired a B.F.A. in Ceramics – though she investigated nearly every department in the school, and tried her hand at many crafts. Upon graduation, she worked at

5. *Flower Vase.* 9 1/2" x 16" long. Polymer clay picture.

her mother's home base, the North Oakland Cultural Art Center's Studio One – teaching ceramics to young and old, and the physically challenged. While teaching these classes, she continued to do her own work concentrating on painting and graphics, as well as on developing her skills as a dancer – her ultimate passion.

Pier's first exposure to the polymer clays was in 1971, during a trip to Germany. She bought a quantity, of the material, brought it back to the States, but did not actually work with it. Instead, she gave it as a gift to a fellow ceramicist. It wasn't until 1978 that she found Fimo™ in a

6. *Window.* 8 1/2" x 16" long. Polymer clay picture.

craft store, was reminded that this material existed, and realized that it might open new areas of exploration for her. Her first products – not surprisingly – were beads. These were made using what might be characterized as "sculptural techniques." The beads were made one-at-a-time, using hand-forming techniques, similar to those used with clay, and not unrelated to "painting," with bits of polymer clay as the "paint." These first beads were made for her own use, and were often given to friends as gifts.

In 1982, Pier moved to New York, where she lived for ten years to pursue a dance career. Because polymer clay

7. *Grey Garden*. 10" x 16 1/2" long.
Polymer clay picture

allows for a relatively simple and compact studio, and because it is in many respects a forgiving and undemanding art material, she was able to continue exploring the use of the material during that time. Pier also thought that making polymer clay jewelry would be an interesting way of supporting herself, since she did not intend to continue teaching. In this period, she began to explore the manufacture of preformed elements – mainly striped canes; and she eventually experimented with creating a cane with an internal pattern – for millefiori work. Having had some exposure to glassworking from her days at CCAC in Oakland, Pier was able to see that polymer clays

8. *Ocean*. 9 1/2" x 16 1/2" long. Polymer clay picture.

could be manipulated in similar ways. At that early period, there were virtually no other artists who were using the material in such complex or intricate ways. While it may not be strictly correct to say she was the first person to comprehend the potential of the material, it would be quite accurate to report that she is one of the true pioneers, who set out to take what was regarded as a "children's toy," and to use it in ways that were artistic, involved and sophisticated.

Pier is the first one to admit that her early creations were not always successful. Like anyone who explores a new medium, and pushes it to its limits, she tried to do things that were not always appropriate –

9. *Yellow and Red Frame*. 10" x 17" long, housing two *Black Bottle Neckpieces*.

things that did not
always work. She
quickly learned what
the technical limits of
the material were, and
what brands were best for
specific applications. In
short order, she began to
develop a personal style,
and to create jewelry unlike
anything else around.

Back in the 1970's,
thousands of tons of old
trade beads from Africa
were imported into the
United States. These were
avidly collected by people
who were interested in
beads – or who became
interested by their
exposure to so many varied
and unusual types. Pier's
mother was such a collector,
and she acquired numerous
beads. Pier can remember
looking at African trade beads
with her mother, and
understanding something
about their manufacture from

10. *Green Leaves*. 10" x 16" long. Polymer clay picture

her exposure to glassworking at school. With this background, in 1984 she began to use Fimo™ to make beads using the more complicated mosaic techniques. She worked mainly from personal intuition, more than from a direct knowledge of glassworking steps and techniques. While old trade beads were inspirational, Pier did not attempt to copy them directly.

When it came to marketing her work, Pier admits that she was in the right place, at the right time, providentially. She first showed her beads to Robert Lee Morris at Artwear. Morris was very encouraging and supportive, and showed her work for about

11. *Flower Frame.* 9" x 16" long, housing a *Floral Bead Neckpiece.*

a year and a half. One day, while on her way to a dance rehearsal, Pier happened across Artisans' Gallery, on Madison Avenue. She made the acquaintance of Julie Schafler Dale, the owner, and found the Gallery was full of beautiful, original, and well-displayed things. Julie was also very encouraging and positive about Pier's work, and enthusiastically accepted Pier's necklaces. Artisans' Gallery was quite successful in selling Pier's work, and continues to be her main outlet in the East. Between 1987 and 1989, Pier danced for choreographer Mark Morris, and no longer had the time to continue making her jewelry. During that period the work of several other artists appeared in New York, and she was intrigued to see their variety of approaches. Suddenly, the polymer clays seemed to become an accepted art material. It is fair to say that

12. *Black, White and Red Frame*. 10" x 12" long, housing a short *Black and White Neckpiece*.

Pier Voulkos was a prime mover in instigating this change in acceptance, by the quality and originality of her work. It is also apparent that she has been an inspiration to other artists who were exposed to her work – though, clearly, artistic people rapidly develop individualistic styles. With the publication of **The New Clay***, it became obvious that a movement had started with this new artist's material!*

When asked how she happened to move away from creating jewelry, Pier said that while she was primarily a beadmaker, she was encouraged by Julie Dale to make earrings to accompany and augment her necklaces. That suggestion led her to a new way of looking at what she was doing, and demanded that she find different ways of putting pieces together, for different functions. Certain gallery owners also suggested that she try her hand at making non-jewelry pieces. Like many

13. *Feather Frame*. 12 1/2" x 12" long, housing a short *Feather Neckpiece*.

14. *Feather Chandelier Earrings*. 3 1/4" long, with stand.

artists, Pier had created larger art objects – and liked the scale and proportion of

such work. Jewelrymaking basically involves small-scale pieces. The polymer clays,

however, can be used for non-jewelry items and for larger-scale pieces. To a great

degree, the formation of Polymer Five had a lot to do with starting the use of polymer

clay for larger art works – not only by Pier, but by the rest of us as well.

Pier had two objectives in creating such work. On the one hand, she intended to

create frames, or settings, in which particular necklaces could be housed and

displayed while not being worn. In addition, she made wall hangings that were

works unto themselves, and did not function to frame jewelry. Both types were shown

in the Five Directions show. They are interesting pieces, in that they are rather

original forms, and feature decorative techniques seldom seen in smaller works.

When asked to discuss her use of the millefiori or caning techniques, and to

15. *Double Harry Earrings.* 2 3/4" long, with stand.

compare this with the larger sculptural pieces, Pier replied that she had integrated the differences and similarities conceptually, and that they relate to past work she had created. Before turning to polymer clay, Pier had been working on large-scale collage pieces, in which she had painstakingly painted the surfaces of papers, cut them into small pieces, and used them to reform large surfaces. When she began making beads, she did not wish to merely copy existing beads from the past – from ancient or historical examples, nor from African trade beads. Instead, she began by making pictorial canes with personal images and over-lapped them so that they formed tiny individual scenes, rather than just covering surfaces with a decorative pattern. In this sense, the beads mirror the collage work she had formerly done with hand-painted paper, though on a much smaller scale. Her larger polymer clay creations reflect aspects of this approach as well, and incorporate some of her techniques using combinations of colors to imitate or suggest decorative stones. One cannot separate result from technique. Initially, these conglomerated colors were

used to make beads that
resembled rocks (either
realistically in tones of black
and white, or in fantasy
colors). Like many artists, Pier
avoided the risk of getting into
a rut by challenging herself
with certain problems – the
solving of which would lead into
new areas of exploration. Her
larger sculptural pieces make
use of conglomerated colors, but
which now have an architectural
quality. She is the first to admit
that she is still at a learning stage
when it comes to the creation of
these works that do not function
as jewelry, are much larger, and
which are displayed in an abstract
setting – a wall. It will be intriguing to see where she
takes it in the future.

    Pier speaks of her involvement with Polymer Five in
terms of enthusiasm and excitement. After several years
of working alone, in an environment that allows one the
peace to explore inner and native creativity, it is
stimulating and challenging to be exposed to the
expression and creativity of other artists working with the
same materials – and who have had similar growth and
evolution.

16. *People Frame.* 13" x 17" long, housing a *People Profile Neckpiece.*

The work of Pier Voulkos may be seen at the following galleries;

- *Julie: Artisans' Gallery, New York, NY.*
- *The Albertson/Peterson Gallery, Winterpark, FL.*
- *Mobilia, Cambridge, MA.*
- *Gallery Eight, La Jolla, CA.*
- *The Virginia Breier Gallery, San Francisco, CA.*
- *Twist Gallery, Portland, OR.*
- *The Giorgi Gallery, Berkeley, CA.*
- *The Hand and the Spirit, Scottsdale, AZ.*

Selected pieces are in the Permanent Collections of:

- *Musée des Arts Decoratiff de Montréal, Montréal, Québec, Canada*
- *The Cooper-Hewitt Museum, of the Smithsonian Institution, in New York City*

17. *Ladder*. 9 1/2" x 18" long. Polymer clay picture.

18. *Wall Clock.* 12" square. Millefiori work on an acrylic base. Martha Breen.

MARTHA BREEN

Martha Breen was born in Chicago, Illinois, on May 21, 1954. She is a life-long artist, and knew at the age of 16 that art would be her calling. In the early years, her major influence was her mother, who taught her the rudiments of drawing. She went to a professional school in England, attended Purdue while still in high-school, and gained a B.F.A. Degree in Printmaking from Indiana University in 1977. She has experimented with various glassworking techniques, and at one time worked as a museum illustrator. Both of these activities made her familiar with traditional glassworking techniques, and she found ancient glass beads particularly fascinating.

Martha's initial discovery of the polymer clays occurred when she bought some at an art store, and played around with it. The material was not very satisfying at first, as she happened to get some stiff, crumbly blocks. She thought of it

19. *Necklace.* 16" long. Spherical millefiori beads with brass findings.

20. *Necklace*, with
matching
earrings and pin.
24" long.
Millefiori work
with brass
findings.

as basically a child's toy, and made fairly simple sculptural pieces from it. Martha occasionally saw articles made from polymer clay – but it was not until her sister Jeni gave her a necklace made by Pier Voulkos that she realized that the medium held the potential to be delicate, expressive and detailed. Prior to this time, and for many years, her graphic art was characterized by almost obsessive use of tiny repeating patterns. She says, "everything was made of patterns." Her familiarity with the glass millefiori technique, and the realization that it could be translated for use with polymer clay, gave her the idea of taking advantage of its potential – allowing her to more easily create the dozens of pattern repetitions she liked using. She showed the necklace made by Pier Voulkos to Michael and Ruth Anne Grove, and thereby stimulated their involvement in the medium as well. For a time, all three would get together and discuss the types of things that might be possible with polymer clay, and experimented with canemaking techniques.

Martha's early canes were not derived from actual beads as much as they were inspired by other influences. She traveled a lot in her childhood, and lived

21. *Pendulum Clock.* 6" x 13" long. Millefiori work on a brass base.

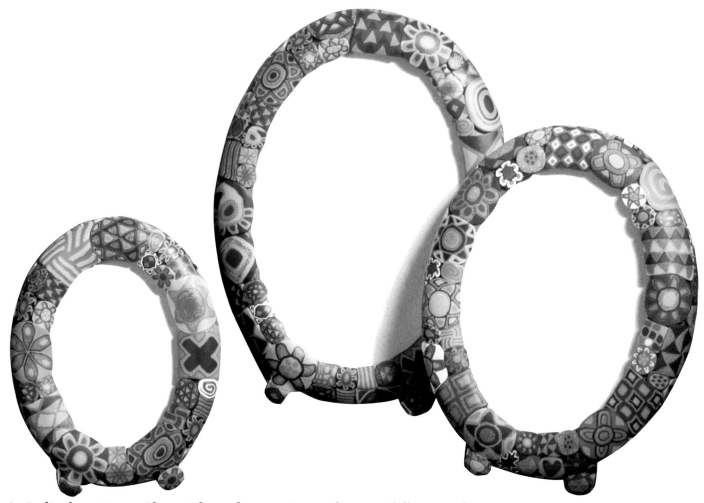

22. *Three Frames*.
Respectively
3 1/2" x 2",
6" x 4", and
5" x 3 1/2"
Millefiori work
on brass
bases, with
glass fronts.

in India for a time. She paid much attention to the way different cultures expressed themselves with colors and patterns. Martha can recall her mother experimenting with batik, and thought this was a marvelous approach to graphic designs. She was always attracted to designs on fabrics – particularly repetitive Indian prints. In her mind, she likes to put geometrical shapes together – and she enjoys creating a unique color palate, by mixing colors together much the same way paints are mixed. One of the main limitations she finds with polymer clay is that the given colors are not true – and often they are too opaque or saturated to have the subtle brilliance of – say, oil paints. This is alleviated by personal color-mixing, and gives an artist a broader and more personal range of choices.

Most of Martha's early constructions were beads that she made and strung into necklaces. The majority of her beads were slices of relatively complicated canes – mostly square or round. These were perforated to become beads, and were often strung alternating with smaller spherical beads. She developed an interesting, but

23. *Wall Clock*. 12" square. Millefiori work on an acrylic base.

uncomplicated style, that has been used by later artists as well. Initially, her goal

was not to turn beadmaking into a business, but was more for enjoyment and

entertainment. By day she was showing her portfolio and looking for work as a

graphic illustrator, and by night was obsessively making canes, and rolling them

out for tiny repeating designs. Little by little, people began to pay more attention to

her clay work than to her graphic art. She came to feel that it might be possible to

produce jewelry, and more-or-less make a living from it.

Although she is something of a miniaturist, and has enjoyed exploiting the nature of canemaking, Martha has grown somewhat tired of the limitations of jewelry manufacture. So, for some time now, she has been experimenting with using the millefiori technique to cover larger surfaces. The first of such works were frames and clocks, which she made at the suggestion of her representative. The initial experiments were disastrous failures. However, one always learns from mistakes – and eventually she devised an approach for producing larger pieces that was effective and successful.

24. *VW Lovebug.* 16" x 8" x 10" wide. Millefiori work on a metal and acrylic base.

These frames were immensely popular. So much so that several other artists have copied them without permission from Martha, and, to their shame, without attribution or credit. Martha proceeded to create clocks and boxes – and many of these current millefiori pieces are made on an acrylic base. Although she admires the larger works done by other artists, such as Michael Grove, she does not have much desire to increase size to this degree. She does not consider herself a sculptress, and doesn't feel that pushing the medium into the creation of truly large-scale works is a natural extension of her personal vision as an artist. She appreciates the ability to use polymer clay for pattern work – which fits her modus operandi. In other respects, Martha feels that it is a limiting medium – and she still works with other materials to find fuller expression of her creativity. Recently, she has returned to working with wood, and with fabric dyes. At a future time, she may devise ways to combine polymer clay with this work.

Martha has a tendency to be somewhat reclusive. She needs a great deal of personal time to draw – or just scribble. She likes to experiment with color combinations. Preparation for work usually involves working out designs on graph paper – which are then translated into canework. On the other hand, she too finds it stimulating to be involved in Polymer Five, and remarks, "what an interesting bunch of people!"

Works by Martha Breen may be seen at:

- *The Museum of American Folk Art, New York, NY.*
- *The Pittsburg Center for the Arts, Pittsburg, PA.*
- *The Chicago Art Institute, Chicago, IL.*
- *The Fabrile Gallery, Chicago, IL.*
- *Chiaroscuro, Chicago, IL.*
- *Mindscape Gallery, Evanston, IL.*
- *Abacus, Booth Bay Harbor, ME.*
- *The Madison Art Center, Madison, WI.*
- *Twist Gallery, Portland, OR.*
- *The Borreti Gallery, San Francisco, CA.*
- *The Scarlet Pallet, Cambria, CA.*
- *New Stone Age, Los Angeles, CA.*

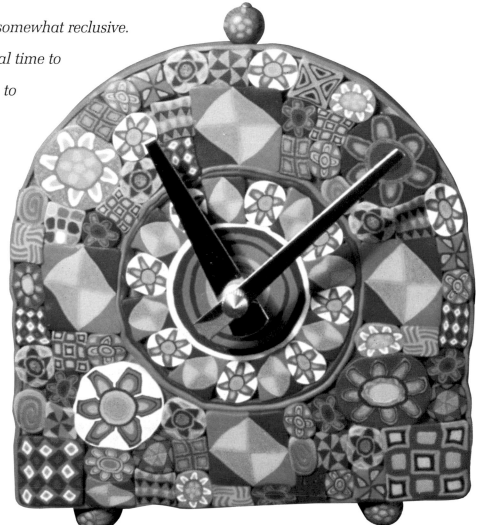

25. *Desk Clock,* 4 1/2" x 5" high. Millefiori work on an acrylic base.

26. *Faces Necklace*. 14"
long. Spheroid millefiori
beads. Ruth Anne Grove.

RUTH ANNE GROVE

Ruth Anne Grove was born in Detroit, Michigan, on October 31, 1936, and grew up in Turrialba, Costa Rica. Her final year of high-school was spent in Ithaca, New York. She graduated from Pomona College in southern California. "Although art and music were not really considered serious courses of study in my family, my mother played piano, was a weaver, and a painter. From her own Turkish bridal cape to pre-Columbian art, she filled our home with beautiful things she had collected

27. *Under Sea Scene*. 6" wide. Barrette with millefiori appliqué collage.

around the world." Because she was not formally trained, Ruth Anne's mother did not consider herself an artist – and this was also Ruth Anne's view of herself for many years. She studied economics and history – "but, what really turned me on were, of course, music and art. I became a singer, and after many years, I began to paint. I stopped being concerned with whether I was or wasn't an artist, and just started doing art! And when that happened, my view of the world became very bright." Her art training consisted of classes in painting and life drawing. She met Michael Grove in the late 1960's in Berkeley, when he was a student at the University of California. They have continued to live in Berkeley, and she has a daughter by a previous marriage.

Twenty five years ago, when her daughter, Frieda,

28. *Shiva and Fashion*. 5" long. Pin with millefiori appliqué collage.

29. *Action, Motion, Movement*. 7" long. Pin with millefiori appliqué collage.

was four, Ruth Anne made
Fimo™ doll-house objects with
her. This new material was
much more satisfying than
Playdough™ or plasticine, was
vibrantly colorful, and easily
baked in a conventional oven.
Years later she began to
understand the artistic
potential of the material when
Martha Breen demonstrated
millefiori canemaking –
calling upon her knowledge of
glassworking techniques.
Upon this renewed
acquaintance with the
material, Ruth Anne quickly
grasped the three-
dimensionality and versatility
of pattern-making. "Working
with Fimo™ that Winter, I
expanded my awareness of its
potential and its problematic
tendencies. By the next
Spring, Michael and I had
created a satisfying group of
necklaces and earrings." They
made a trip to New Orleans
that May, to attend the

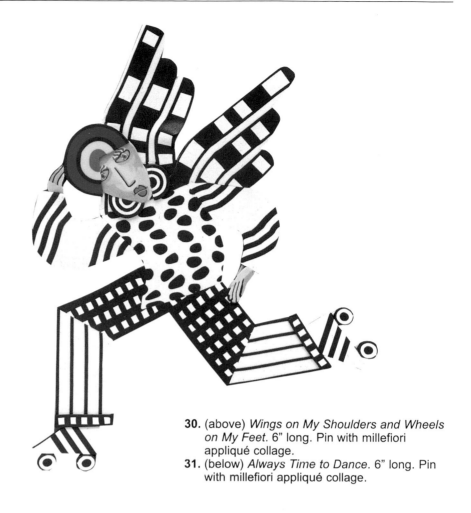

30. (above) *Wings on My Shoulders and Wheels on My Feet*. 6" long. Pin with millefiori appliqué collage.
31. (below) *Always Time to Dance*. 6" long. Pin with millefiori appliqué collage.

Heritage Jazz Festival, and took their new jewelry with them, to see if they could peddle it around the French Quarter. Some days later, walking down Royale Street, they stopped in a local store to show their wares. They were turned down. However, the next store took everything they had. With this beginning, she and Michael began to produce polymer clay art for sale. They entered the wholesale market, first in San Francisco, and then in New York, finding their way experimentally and intuitively. "The experience was terrifying and exhilarating, and propelled us into a new life."

Within her art, Ruth Anne works almost exclusively in the millefiori technique. Initially, she constructed canes in which a single slice provided an entire complex image, scene, or situation. Although this is a valid procedure, often used by polymer clay artists, and which

32. *Dressed to Wear.* 5" long. Earrings with millefiori appliqué collage.

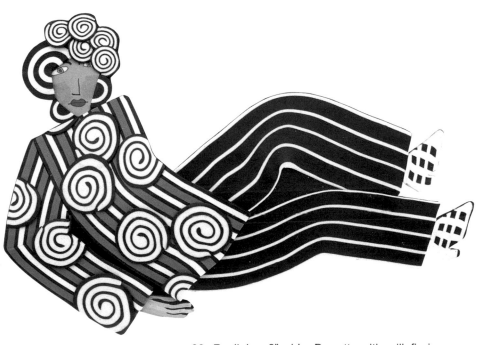

33. *Reclining.* 6" wide. Barrette with millefiori appliqué collage.

necessitates certain kinds of problem solving, Ruth Anne felt it was somewhat limiting. Instead, she turned to making separate canes that would provide different parts of a desired scene, and used slices of these to produce individual creations similar to collage work. She is excited and stimulated by this "appliqué" approach. Currently, many of the beads she is making are constructed in this manner as well. Her pins are often stylized highly-graphic animated figures. Her ability to express movement or activity – for instance in her skaters – gives the work a virtuosity that is charming and impressive. "They represent for me an unrealistic kind of realism."

When asked about her artistic relationship to Michael, it becomes clear that their work is truly the result of a collaboration. Ruth Anne is

34. (above) *Rolling into the Present.* 5" long. Pin with millefiori appliqué collage.
35. (below) *If Only We Had Time.* 6" long. Pin with millefiori appliqué collage.

more likely to refer to
Michael as her 'partner,'
rather than her
'husband.' They both
make and share canes,
and almost any finished
product may have
components from both
partners. Michael is a

36. *Earrings.* 2" long. Millefiori appliqué collage.

great catalyst for Ruth Anne. She remarks, "I am
constantly surprised and astonished with Michael's work.
He chooses colors sometimes from another planet, and I find
myself seeing colors in a new way."

When asked about her feelings regarding the formation
of Polymer Five, Ruth Anne said, "I am privileged to be a
part of the forefront of this growing movement. The show
encouraged me to push the limits of the medium – and
the people in this group
dazzle and inspire me.
They are a large part of
the excitement of this life
that we have hurled
ourselves into."

For gallery listings,
refer to page 41.

37. *Earrings.* 2" long. Millefiori appliqué collage.

38. *Inside Outside.* 6" wide. Barrette with millefiori appliqué collage.

39. *Fashion and Fusion.* 2 1/2" wide. Two pins in a series of six, with millefiori appliqué collage.

40. *Thorny Vines*. 10" x 14" long. Picture with millefiori appliqué collage. Michael Grove.

MICHAEL GROVE

Michael Grove was born in Oakland, California, on January 19, 1949, and is a life-long resident of Berkeley. His art training revolved around

41. *Not-a-Vessel #7*. 14" tall. Black vessel with multipatterned interior, on a loose stalk base.

ceramics. In the late 1960's he met and married Ruth Anne, while he was a student at the University of California. In 1973 he was the chief assistant to the ceramics teacher at Merrit College – where he helped advanced students, mixed glazes, and fired up the kilns.

He is otherwise self-taught, and has been a
productive artist since 1970. Between
1980 and 1983, Michael contrived
to build a thirty-five cubic foot
kiln in his backyard, and
worked out of a home studio.
He loved all aspects of
ceramics, and could not
settle down to one style or
area of production – but tried
everything. He says, "I reveled
in the endless possibilities – from
gritty, rough and course texture, to
translucence." After several years of
this, he realized that he wasn't finding
a niche in ceramics, wouldn't be able
to continue in the profession – and
decided it was time to leave his
studio.

   Attending Laney College
in Oakland, Michael
studied computer
science, and was
getting fairly steady
work as a computer
consultant. "I thought I
was through with making
things. Working as an artist
again was definitely not part

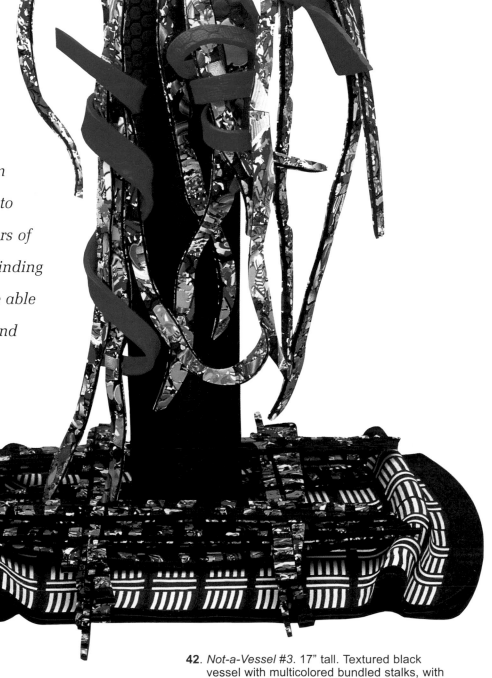

42. *Not-a-Vessel #3*. 17" tall. Textured black
vessel with multicolored bundled stalks, with
loose multicolored stalks on a black and white
patterned base.

of my plans." One day in 1986, while visiting Martha

Breen, he and Ruth Anne were shown an impressive

necklace. It happened that Martha's sister, Jeni, was a

dancer in the same company as Pier Voulkos, and had

acquired one of Pier's necklaces. They were

all dazzled by this

intriguing piece of

jewelry, and were

provoked to discuss its nature

and technique.

Michael immediately

became enamored with the

material, noticing that it had

much in common with clay. It

was a tactile substance that one

could sculpt and manipulate. He

realized it had enormous possibility

for endless variety of expression and

use. In contrast to ceramic clay,

polymer clay was a

compact,

neat, and orderly medium, that required less technology

and equipment. "I spent all my spare time late into the

evening unraveling its mysteries and marvels, inventing

43. *Not-a-Vessel #4*. 15" tall. Yellow vessel with black and white circles, on a black and white base with black and white circles.

techniques and developing effects." His one reservation

was that it was more suitable for small-scale work and

did not seem

appropriate

for larger

pieces. He

created

jewelry for a

while, but

also began to

contemplate the

possibilities of more

massive constructions.

"Making wearable pieces

has allowed me to develop

techniques for

polymer

44. *Not-a-Vessel #1.* 15" tall.
Textured red vessel, with blue
and yellow stalks, on a textured
black base.

clay that I now apply to larger work, and vice versa."

The texturing of patterns in his 'Not-a-Vessel' series

inspired his 'Cosmic Curiosity' pin series.

In discussing his partnership with Ruth Anne, Michael

remarks that they are so integrally connected that their

work, as a whole, must be considered a collaboration.

"Even when we work apart, we consult so frequently and

are so influenced by the other's aesthetic that our combined threads become a seamless part of each piece." On most of their jewelry, both their names appear regardless who may have done what. This is liberating and fulfilling work not limited by jealousy, reserve, or the sense that there is any need to hold back. They enjoy sharing and using each others ideas. Michael says, "It's a yeasty, fermentative, buoyant, playful exchange..., a rare kind of freedom – a special relationship."

45. *Not-a-Vessel #2.* 15" tall. Textured red vessel, blue stalks with black and white circles, on a blue base with black and white circles.

    Michael found the millefiori technique extremely intriguing. He enjoyed the technical aspect of creating an image within a cane, on a large scale – and then reducing it by rolling and stretching, to make it a very small-scale image. Along with Ruth Anne, he enjoyed seeing how small the image could be made, without losing its pictorial integrity, or what quirky effect could be created by manipulating the patterns. He concentrated on making earrings, and soon began to incorporate mixed media effects – experimenting by wrapping pieces with wire, and with adding metallic elements. Out of a desire to have a larger surface to work with, he began to make necklaces, allowing bolder patterns with a crisp, graphic look that stood out strikingly from a distance.

By the end of the first year, he began to explore the possibility of making non-jewelry pieces. He attempted to compose a box using his experience with woodworking, but quickly grasped that the 'wood solution' for joining and detailing was not appropriate for polymer clay. It took about three weeks to create something that didn't self-destruct! The first boxes

46. *Not-a-Vessel #5.* 16" tall. Black vessel with flowing blue multicolored stalks, pierced by multicolored stalks, on a multicolored blue base.

were plain-colored inside, and patterned outside. In short order, he placed contrasting patterns on the exterior and interior. The outside was orderly, while the interior was wild and spontaneous – a feature that surprised and delighted people who would examine and open the boxes. Michael was invited to participate in a show called 'Time and Reflections,' for which he made mirrors framed with polymer clay. "This was my first shot at combining my interest in deconstructive philosophy with my polymer clay art. A continuous loop with music and voice-over played endlessly along the shattered wall mirror spouting phrases like 'time is money, save time, lose time, make time, do time.'" He has continued to frame mirrors with polymer clay patterns, constructing

47. *Not-a-Vessel #6.* 14" tall. Red striped vessel with blue interior stripes, on a multicolored base.

remarkably complex and original pieces.

Michael conceived the idea of a group show when Pier Voulkos wandered into his booth at an art show in Berkeley. Pier had just moved back to the Bay Area from New York City. He had also repeatedly heard of Jamey Allen's reputation, while participating in art shows around the country. "At that time, the few people around the country who had any discriminating understanding of polymer clay had somehow taken a workshop with Jamey. He is a scholar, educator, and artist." With the addition of Martha Breen, Michael realized five innovative, nationally-known artists were now living and working in the Bay Area around San Francisco. Possibilities for doing something together dazzled him. When the Polymer Five show was proposed, we all agreed that it was important to produce items that pushed the medium beyond jewelry, and other items we had made before.

Having long been involved in vesselmaking, Michael wanted to use polymer clay in a similar manner, but realized that a polymer clay version might not be as functional as ceramic ones. So, using the general conformation of containers he invented the "Not-a-Vessel," a vase-shaped art object for display and enjoyment. Since "Not-a-Vessels" were not water tight, and couldn't hold flowers in the conventional manner, Michael proceeded to make

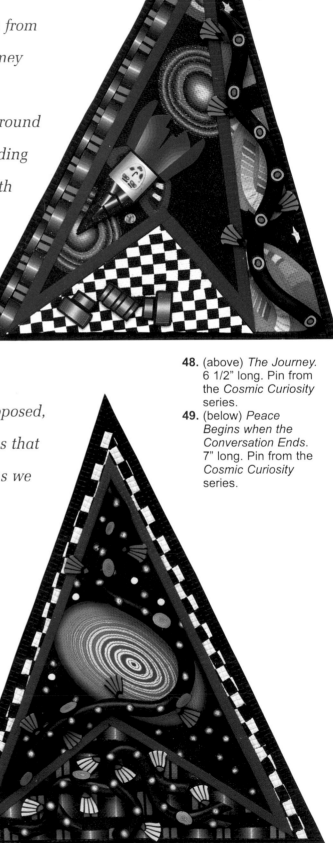

48. (above) *The Journey.* 6 1/2" long. Pin from the *Cosmic Curiosity* series.

49. (below) *Peace Begins when the Conversation Ends.* 7" long. Pin from the *Cosmic Curiosity* series.

interesting stalk-like constructions to take the place of flowers. The effect of these objects is startlingly otherworldly and mysterious. They not only take a conventional form and make it unconventional – they also feature interesting juxtapositions of patterned versus plain surfaces, and textured versus smooth surfaces. A verbal description is insufficient. They must be seen to really appreciate their originality.

Michael is the backbone of Polymer Five, in the sense that he does a lot of the organizational work for the rest of us. He has managed to guide us without dictating, and

50. (above) *Heart and Heat.* 3" x 4" wide. Pin with miliefiori appliqué collage.
51. (below) *By the Sea.* 3 1/2" x 3 1/2" wide. Pin with millefiori appliqué collage.

leads us to make decisions by consensus. He says the process of developing the group and pulling the show together has been a delight and an inspiration. We know it has also been a source of anxiety and consternation, at certain moments. Michael deserves and has our gratitude.

52. (above) *Another Unintelligible Commentary on the Incomprehensible.* 5" x 6" wide. Pin from the *Cosmic Curiosity* series.

53. (below) *Heart Felt Delivery.* 5" long. Pin with background prop in millefiori appliqué collage.

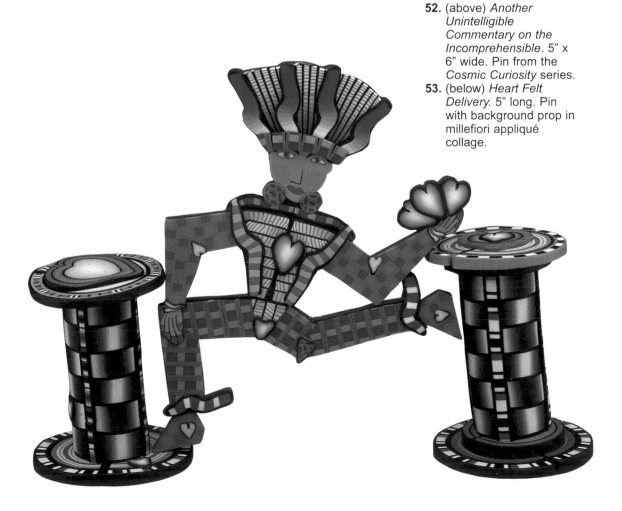

Works by Michael and Ruth Anne Grove may be seen at the following galleries:

- *The Giorgi Gallery, Berkeley, CA.*
- *The Flying Shuttle, Seattle, WA.*
- *The Hanson Gallery, Houston, TX.*
- *The Pittsburg Museum Gallery, Pittsburg, PA.*
- *Julie: Artisans' Gallery, New York, NY.*
- *Mobilia, Cambridge, MA.*
- *The Pittsburgh Center for the Arts, Pittsburg, PA.*

Selected pieces are in the Permanent Collection of:

- *The Cooper-Hewitt Museum, of the Smithsonian Institution, in New York City.*

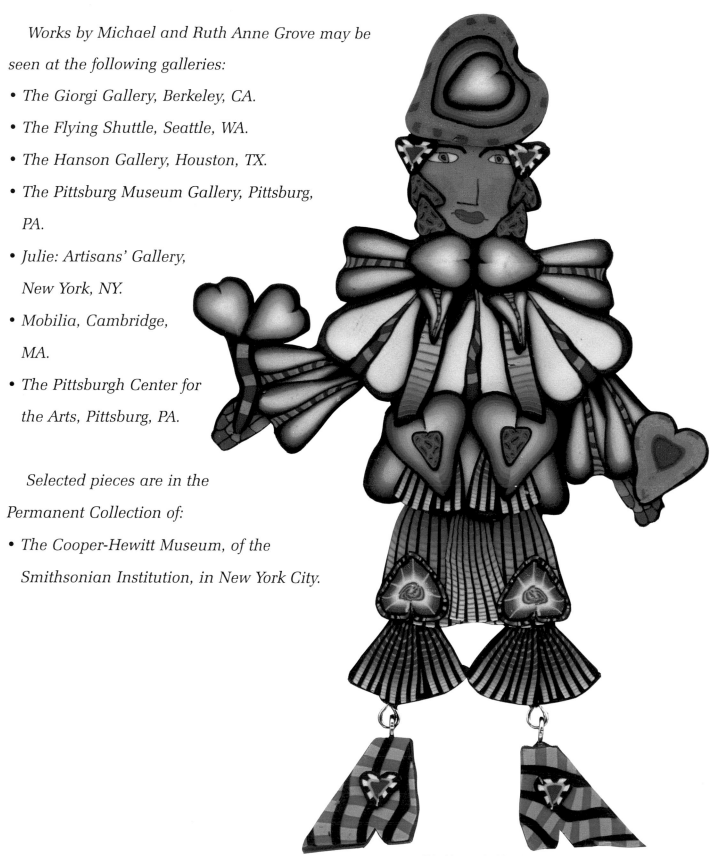

54. *Hearts in Hand and Everywhere Else.* 6" long. Pin with millefiori appliqué collage.

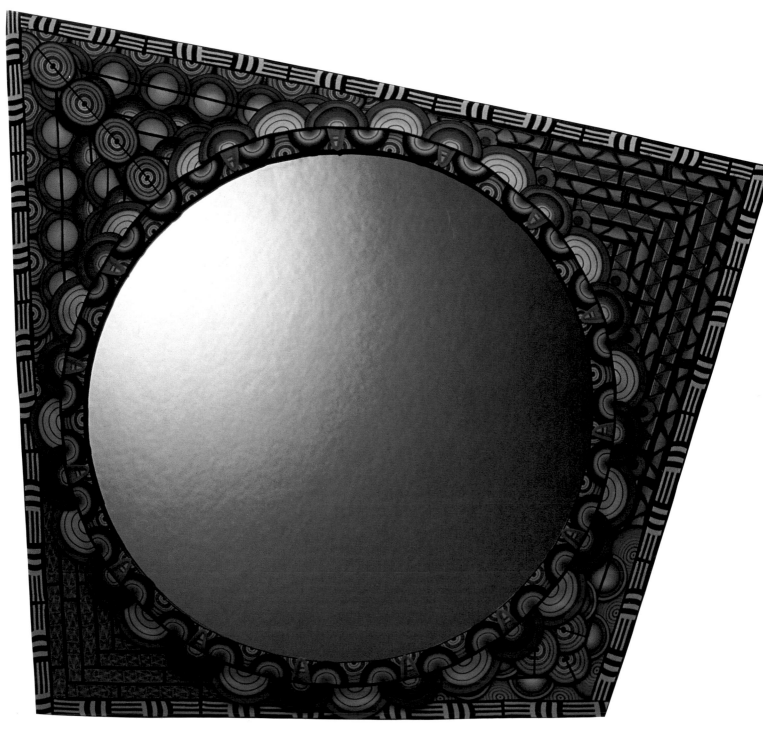

55. *Mirror with Round Center.* 17" x 19" long.
Millefiori appliqué collage.

56. *Mirror with Asymmetrical Center.* 17" x 19"
long. Millefiori appliqué collage.

Ruth Anne & Michael Grove

57. (above) *At the Gallery.* 11" x 18" wide. Polymer clay picture. Ruth Anne and Michael Grove.

58. (right) *Which Way? This Way.* 10" x 14" long. Polymer clay picture.

59. *Two Necklaces.* Combed Pond folded beads, in tones of black, white, and gray. Crown-knotted on black braided lines, with button or toggle closures. Jamey Allen.

JAMEY D. ALLEN

60. Section of a necklace of combed and folded beads, in tones of pink, black, and gray. Crown-knotted on pink braided lines.

I was born on March 19, 1951, in Bremerton, Washington, have lived in California since the age of two, and in the Bay Area since 1962. I have considered myself an artist since I was six – though through the years I have had many interests and potential career goals. I have dabbled in all major art media, from painting and sculpture, to weaving, needlework, soft sculpture, quilting, collage, and photography. In addition, I have tried my hand in the field of performance as a singer, dancer, and actor within community theater. All these interests have contributed to my life as an artist in meaningful and surprising ways. My involvement with

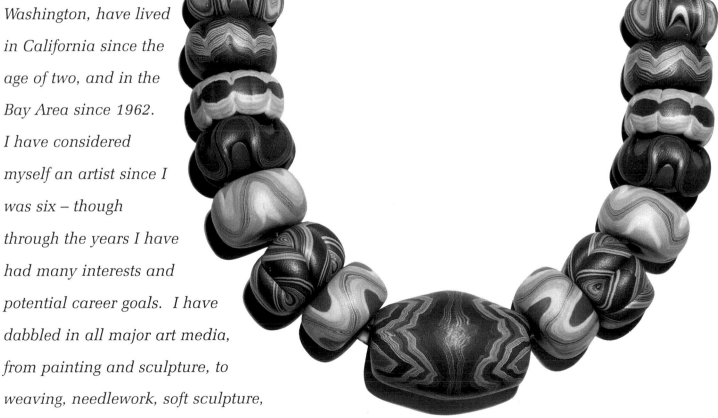

61. The same necklace as above, prior to knotting and closure.

beads began in 1967, with the breakdown of traditional sex-role stereotyping – a time when it became OK for men to have long hair, unusual clothes, and to wear jewelry. As there was no men's jewelry to speak of, I invented it. It is an understatement to say I am a nonconformist! I've always felt like a unicorn in a herd of horses. In working with beads, I primarily did intricate beadwork for the first five years. However, all this occurred at a time when an explosion of bead importing was beginning. In 1970, when I moved to San Francisco, I was near The Bead Store. I worked there for a year in 1972–and was a daily fixture in the store for over ten years. The abundance of beads – particularly American Indian and African trade beads – fascinated me. I became quite interested in their history and technical nature. Unavoidably, I heard a lot of tales about beads that were interesting, but didn't sound like real history. By 1974, I began to study beads avidly, and began my first attempt at writing something meaningful about them. My interest has not been limited to any particular type or variety of beads. I am a bead generalist – someone who studies beads of all periods, cultural origins, and materials. Through the years, however, I have made particular studies

62. Bolo Tie. About 1 5/8" wide. Depicting an Echinocerius cactus in bloom. Millefiori work, suspended from a braided plastic cord with millefiori terminals.

of beads made of organic materials, ancient and modern glass bead technology, and beads made of synthetic materials. In 1977, I was a founding member of the Northern California Bead Society – the second of such organizations anywhere in the world. (There are now over thirty.) While pursuing these interests, I have supported myself primarily by selling my bead creations, and by taking individual commissions from collectors and gallery owners. For twenty-six years, hardly a day has gone by in which I have not had my hands on beads, or bead-related studies and

63. Four Millefiori Pins. About 1 3/4" wide. Depicting (clockwise): an Echinocerius cactus in bloom; a Maenad (a traditional Greek figure); an ear of Indian blue corn; and an Echinocerius cactus in a desert scape.

pursuits. Along with publishing about beads, I have also
developed into a public speaker with an international
schedule of speaking engagements. Most recently, I have
become a teacher.

    In dealing with ancient glass beads, the most
technically challenging aspect concerns theories of how
they may have been manufactured. Because I am not
expert in glasswork, but am more abstractly
knowledgeable, I haven't had much opportunity to
conduct tangible experiments to prove or disprove my
ideas. In 1984, I began to hear about polymer clay, first
from a friend who thought it would be a good medium for

64. *Rorschach Plate.* About 5"
wide. Millefiori dish in tones
of black and white, with
reversing patterns on each
surface.

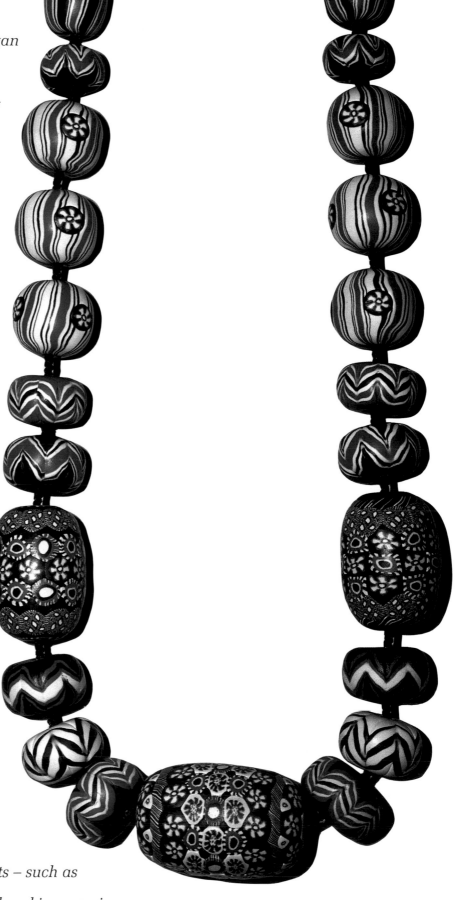

experimentation. In 1987, I began working with Fimo™. Initially, my intention was to make a few beads, have some fun, and see what I could discover than might have ramifications toward traditional or historical glass beadmaking. Amazingly, I discovered the medium was both challenging and rewarding in ways I didn't suspect might be the case. Although through the years I developed skills that allowed me to work creatively with existing beads from around the world, I was not basically a beadmaker. Once I was able to take a material and form my own beads and components, I experienced a satisfaction and fulfillment that I hadn't realized was missing from my life as an artist.

After a few experiments with duplicating hand-formed products – such as Phoenician head pendants – and making a series of millefiori canes and beads, I turned to

65. Necklace of floral millefiori and combed beads, in tones of black, white, and gray. Crown-knotted on black nylon lines. Collection of Patricia Nulph.

intriguing glass beads that had not been duplicated by other artists. The most appealing of these were the so-called "folded beads," thought to have been made in the environs of the Persian Empire, over 1,000 years ago. Having carefully examined and photographed many examples of these beads, and by diagramming their structure, I was able to devise a plan for making polymer clay beads that would replicate them. No glass artist has been able to accomplish this, so far; and no polymer clay artist had been exposed to folded beads for inspiration prior to my reinvention. I have taught almost 1,000 beadmakers to do this work! I first presented these beads for a wider audience in Nan Roche's book, **The New Clay**. By now, folded beads have become a popular and unique approach to making polymer clay beads - and I am proud to have devised this; as well as reinventing other ancient glassworking practices that yield unusual beads when worked in the material.

I continue to try to duplicate intricate glass beads from times past, using polymer clay, but my work is not confined to this. Having learned the skills of glassworking, and translated them into working with polymer clay, I take these skills and now make beads that are unique to me. Except where they clearly copy historical examples, my beads are a "new animal" in the bead world. Like my

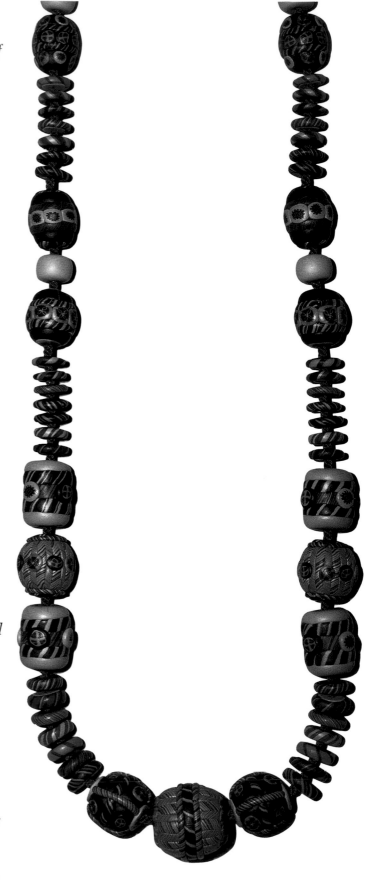

66. Necklace of millefiori and twisted candy-cane beads, in tones of violet, yellow, and brown. Crown-knotted on nylon lines.

friends in Polymer Five, I have discovered

that man does not live by beads alone –

and I make a variety of other

products as well. Needless to

say, until recently I have

not strayed far from the

category of personal

adornment, and

mostly make

pendants,

earrings, pins,

bracelets, and

barrettes.

When I made

the acquaintance of

Michael and Ruth

Anne Grove, in 1992, I

was already considering

expanding the medium beyond

its use for body adornment, and to

make other art objects. In the first

meetings we had for the Five Directions in Polymer show,

we agreed that we would try to present new and divergent

works. For my part, I decided to experiment with making

vessels, based primarily on ancient glass prototypes. To

this end, I have created small vases and shallow bowls,

derived from the repertoire of ancient Middle Eastern

glassworkers. I am still perfecting the construction of

these, and considering further steps or elaborations, and

67. *Pomegranate Vase.* 3 1/2" tall. Hollow, with striped and combed decoration, in tones of red, black, and white. The form copies glass prototypes, nearly 4,000 years old.

*additional products or forms.
Like any artist, I want my art to be
unique, and to make a personal
statement. However, no one
works in a vacuum for very
long – and few people can
avoid influence and
inspiration from their peer
group (and probably
shouldn't try too hard). My
normal modus operandi,
when I see someone else making
a particular style or form is to avoid
it like the plague, unless I'm already
involved in it. There are many
competent polymer clay artists
creating work that I admire,
but have no desire to emulate.
My four friends and I in
Polymer Five make up a
unique and interesting group.
We are not merely a "mutual
admiration society," although we
truly do admire one another, find
inspiration in joining together, and
continue to push the medium in ways that
remain individualistic. To me, it is
astounding that this can happen – and happen so easily.
I feel blessed to be in such good company; and I hope*

68. Necklace of Persian folded beads. In tones of ochre, cream and gray. Crown-knotted on ochre braided nylon lines, with a button closure. Collection of Ruth Shine.

readers of this publication enjoy it as a document of the work we have done and presented together in our first showing.

Jamey D. Allen works primarily on an individual commission basis, rather than through ongoing association with galleries and institutions. However, his work may be viewed at the Giorgi Gallery, 2911 Claremont Ave., Berkeley, CA. He may be contacted directly at: P. O. Box 1582, Santa Rosa, CA. 95402-1582.

69 Detail of a necklace of Persian folded and millefiori, and sterling beads, with a square millefiori pendant inlaid in handmade sterling. The pendant is about 2 1/4" square. In tones of green, and crown-knotted on green nylon lines.

70. Necklace of millefiori, folded, and combed beads. In tones of red, black, white, and gray. Strung with black horn filler beads, with a button closure.